Dread and Splendor

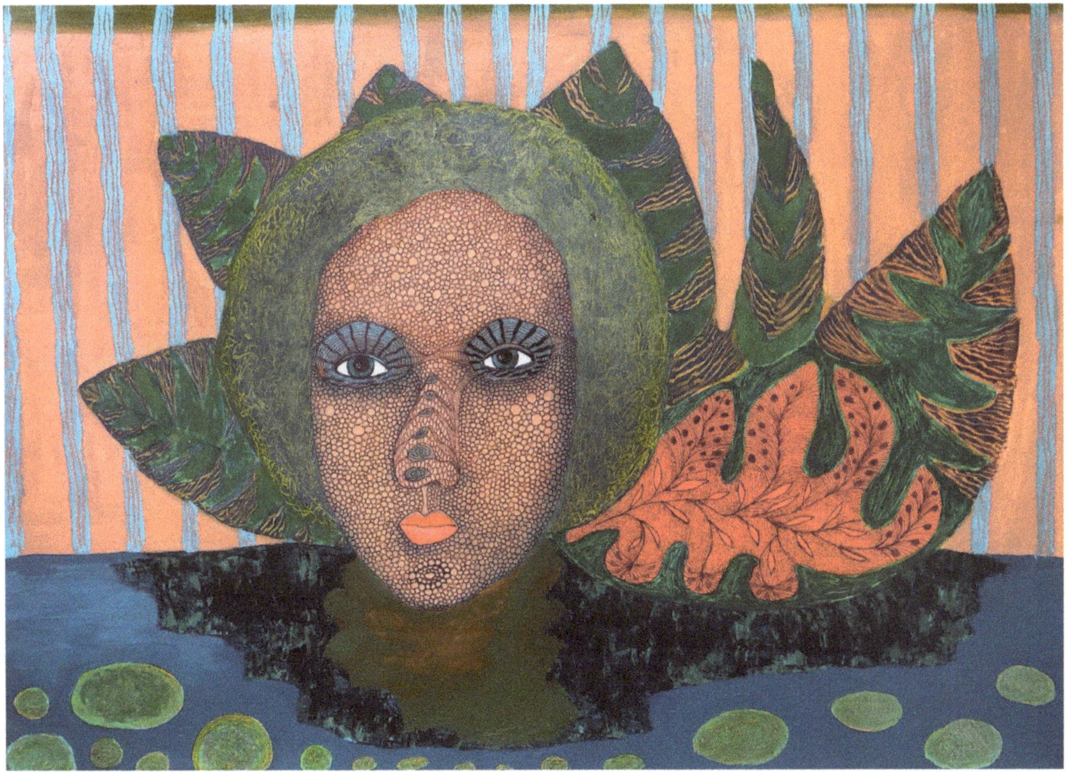

I Feel Close to Nature Too
Acrylic and Ink on Paper, 20" x 30"

Dread and Splendor

Paintings and Poems for a New Earth

art by **Irene Christensen**
poetry by **Eileen P. Kennedy**

SHANTI ARTS PUBLISHING

BRUNSWICK, MAINE

Dread and Splendor:
Paintings and Poems for a New Earth

Published by Shanti Arts Publishing

Designed by Shanti Arts Designs

Shanti Arts LLC
193 Hillside Road
Brunswick, Maine 04011
shantiarts.com

Printed in the United States of America

ISBN: 978-1-962082-81-5 (softcover)

Library of Congress Control Number: 2025944582

This book is dedicated to the women at the heart of the environmental movement who struggle to keep our earth safe.

Special thanks from Eileen to Carla Cooke, Jane McPhetres Johnson, Eugene Tencza, Cheryl J. Fish, Ellen D. Coleman.

Contents

Acknowledgments / 11
Foreword / 13
Introduction / 15

Metamorphosis / 18
Metamorphosis / 19

My Dancing Dream / 20
My Dancing Dream / 21

Daydreamers / 22
Daydreamers / 23

Dreaming Venice / 24
Dreaming Venice / 25

Lotus Dreamer / 26
Lotus Dreamer / 27

Guardian of Dreams / 28
Guardian of Dreams / 29

Deer Guardian / 30
Deer Guardian / 31

Mindscape of the Night / 32
Mindscape of the Night / 33

The Day Wavers between Going and Staying / 34
The Day Wavers between Going and Staying / 35

Young Woman / 36
To Be That Young / 37

Yesterday / 38
She Occupies Time / 39

Child of 1000 Years / 40
What World Will We Leave Her? / 41

Perilous Journey / 42
Perilous Journey / 43

The Blue Line / 44
Blue Line / 45

Red Wall / 46
The Red Wall / 47

Nature Remains Our Home / 48
Nature Is Our Home / 49

I Feel Close to Nature Too / 50
The Closeness of Nature / 51

Māori Woman / 52
Māori / 53

Queen of the Woods / 54
Queen of the Woods / 55

Wandering Queen / 56
Wandering Queen / 57

Artemis / 58
Artemis / 59

Lotus Goddess / 60
Lotus Goddess / 61

The Goddess Speaks / 62
The Goddess Speaks / 63

Ino / 64
Ino and the Goddesses / 65

Between Shell and Troll / 66
Between Shell and Troll / 67

Looking to the Future / 68
The Eyes Have It / 69

About the Artist and Poet / 71

Acknowledgments

Arlington Literary Journal: "The Day Wavers Between Going and Coming" (August 1, 2024) https://www.arlijo.com/post/issue-200#viewer-huuwn650

Ekphrastic Review: "Between Shell and Troll"/*Between Shell and Troll;* "The Goddess Speaks" / *The Goddess Speaks;* "Ino and the Goddesses"/*Ino;* "Lotus Goddess" / *Lotus Goddess;* and "Māori"/*Māori Woman* (January 11, 2024)

Starry Starry Kite: "Daydreams"/*Daydreams;* "I Feel Close to Nature Too"/*I Feel Close to Nature Too;* and "Māori"/*Māori Woman* (August 13, 2023) https://starrystarrykite.substack.com

Wordpeace: "Perilous Journey"/*Perilous Journey* (Winter, 2025)

"My Dancing Dream"/*Dancing Dream* were exhibited at HERSTORY: The Battle Continues: An Exhibition for All Genders; Viridian Artists, 548 West 28th Street, New York City (February 20–March 16, 2024)

"Perilous Journey"/*Perilous Journey* were exhibited at the Peaceable Kingdom Exhibition; The Interchurch Center, 61 Claremont Avenue, New York City (November 20, 2023–January 4, 2024); published in *Wordpeace* (Winter 2025)

"Queen of the Woods"/*Queen of the Woods* were exhibited at Voices of Earth Exhibition, Galleri Schaeffers Gate 5, Schaeffers Gate 5, 0558 Oslo, Norway (June 15–18, 2022) http://schaeffersgate5.no

Foreword

by GINGER ANDRO
Artist, Curator, and Vice President,
Sculptors Guild, New York City

I met Irene Christensen's paintings first at the Ringwood Manor
Galleries and again at her solo show at the Bergen County Museum
soon after I moved to northern New Jersey. I made a point of meeting
her personally as I desperately needed to meet another serious
working artist living in the "burbs." Her work was colorful, lyrical,
powerful, and deeply moving. The natural, well-articulated marks of
the paint demonstrated a profoundly intuitive connection between
artist and medium through a unique painting language that utilizes the
architecture, geography, and mythology of her native Norway. Irene's
paintings seem to contain her personality, her balanced optimism, and
love of nature.

I have had the pleasure of working with Irene for nonprofit art
organizations—selecting, curating, and organizing shows as members
of the gallery committee for the Zakin Gallery and currently as board
members of the Sculptors Guild in New York City. We have shown
together in many exhibits. I am forever grateful for our association as
fellow artists. I know her fine work, and I call Irene a friend.

For years, Irene Christensen participated in the residency program
at the Julia and David White Artists' Colony in Costa Rica. It is there
that she met award-winning poet Eileen Kennedy. Eileen has authored
two collections: *Banshees* (Flutter Press, 2015) and *Touch My Head
Softly* (Finishing Line Press, 2021). The Colony, situated in a private
seventeen-acre rainforest, offers artists the privilege of exploring

the lush and volatile landscape, encountering exotic wildlife, and delving into the rich pre-Columbian history and cultural heritage. Costa Rica, with its unwavering commitment to conservation and sustainability, has turned much of its tropical paradise into protected parks and reserves. These two artists soon discovered their shared passion for the living world and dedication to preserving our precious planet. During this immersive residency, they also recognized their mutual awareness of a parallel between nature and the feminine, both possessing an inherent strength and resilience.

It was in Costa Rica that Eileen gave Irene the poetry book *Touch My Head Softly* and was given the painting *Volcano Flower* in response, initiating the conversation that resulted in *Dread and Splendor: Paintings and Poems for a New Earth*. A collection of Eileen's ekphrastic poems were written in response to Irene's surrealistic paintings, creating a collaboration between two accomplished women that joins their individual art forms to create a many-leveled connection to hearts and minds. This is a unique and important book for our troubled times, offering insight and healing.

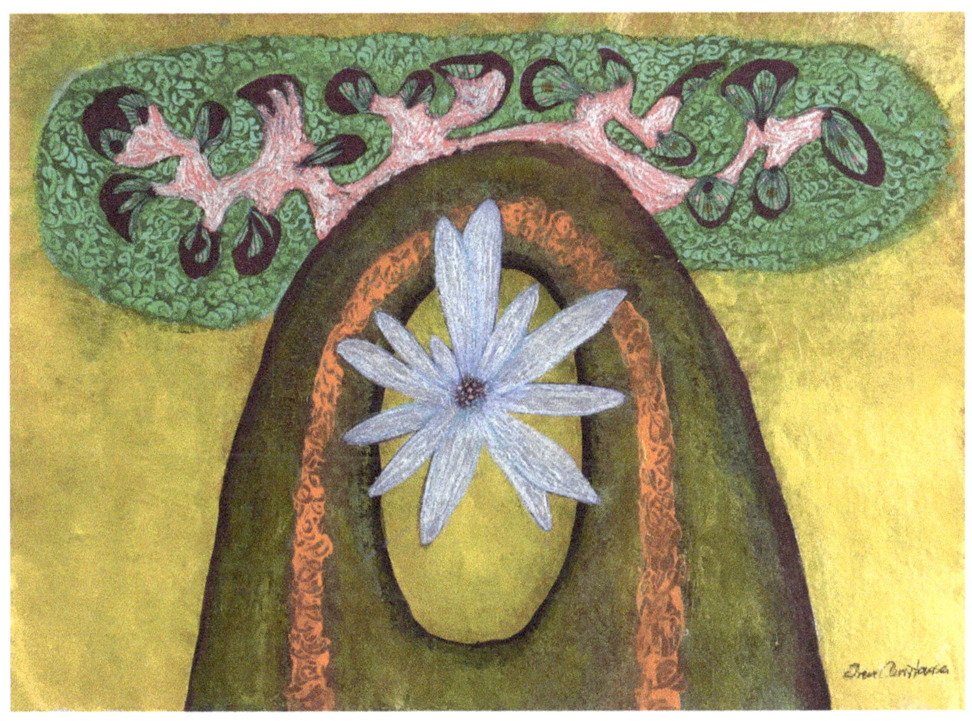

Volcano Flower
Acrylic on Handmade Paper, 8.5" x 12"

Introduction

Another world is not only possible, she is on her way.
—ARUNDHATI ROY, Author and Political Activist

Irene Christensen, a Norwegian artist, and Eileen P. Kennedy, an American poet, met years ago at The David and Julia White Artists' Colony in Ciudad Colón, Costa Rica. They both loved this biologically spectacular country. When Eileen gave Irene a copy of her book *Touch My Head Softly*, Irene reciprocated with her painting *Volcano Flower*, painted at Arenal Volcano—part of their shared experience.

Dread and Splendor: Paintings and Poems for a New Earth
comes from their common interest in natural beauty, the complex
relationship between living things and the atmosphere, the stopping
of exploitation of the earth that spans geographical and historical
borders, and the feminine care at the center of environmentalism.

Irene worked on a series of art pieces over the years about women and
the impact of the climate on the world. Eileen, observing the creation
of these remarkable paintings, wrote a series of ekphrastic poems,
or written responses, to them. The artist and poet nurtured their
creativity and friendship through this process.

Irene's paintings unfold as the world heats up and becomes more
and more unlivable. She creates images through the eyes of children,
perspectives of mythical characters like trolls and goddesses, and the
lenses of women witnessing the globe dying. Eileen reinforces this
journey in words, giving verbal credence to Irene's vision of the future.

The book is many layered. It's a vehicle for looking inward to a place
where you may see choices for the world more clearly. Images from
all over—Norway, Costa Rica, the United States—depict a planet at a
pivotal moment, when wild places and refuges are deteriorating.

You'll meet yourself mirrored in the spaces where these poems and
paintings intersect. Like a chilling wind creeping from flower to
flower, the beauty of the paintings and poetry stand in stark contrast
to the bleak message they convey. In stunning visuals and provocative
words, the book provides a haunting view of the forthcoming globe.
In *Dread and Splendor*, artist and poet cast a light on the passing of
the earth, the role of women in trying to prevent it, and the hope for
environmental preservation in a newly envisioned world.

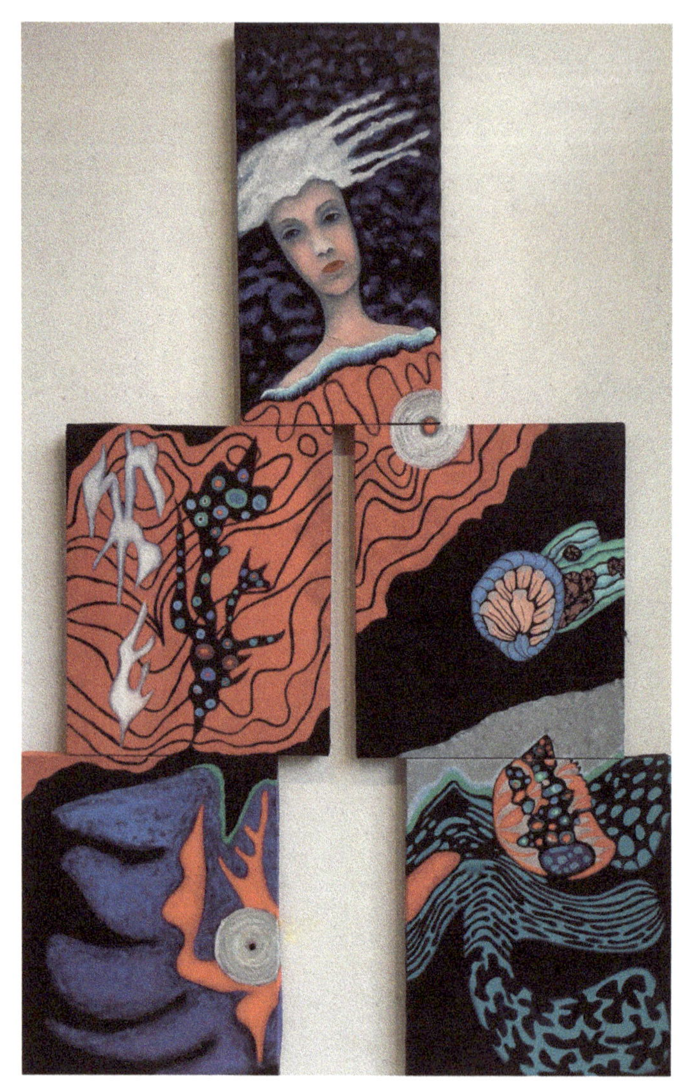

Metamorphosis
Oil, 64" x 39"

Metamorphosis

Celebrating red pearls
lingering in pink shells

the woman transforms.
Her beauty enhances wildlife

in plants and ocean
in distinct parts.

She dissects the earth
cuts it open

like a corpse.
Her head in water
her body grounded in earth.
She holds the configuration
the shells   the sea nymphs.
Unable to swim the vast divide

she changes to the Tethys Ocean
ancient water
apart and adrift.

She keeps the old sea's secrets
in the depths hidden unseen
the waves cry out for relief
as the mysteries convene.

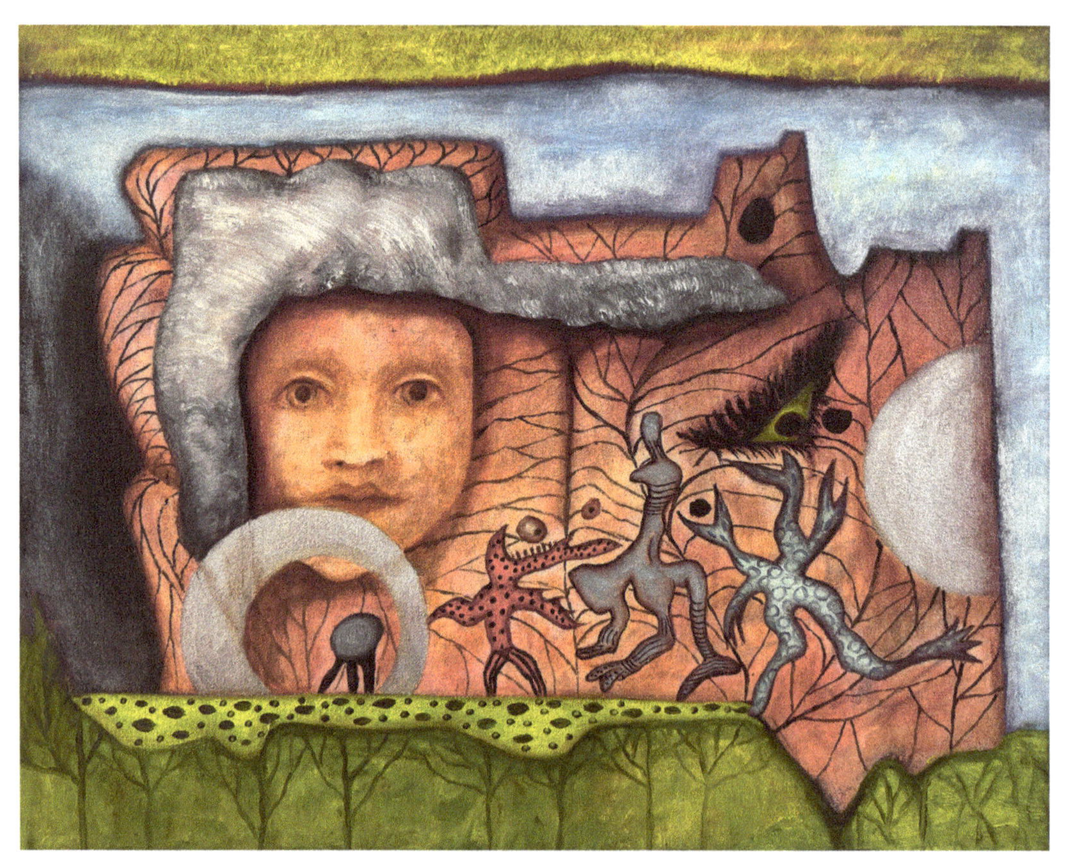

My Dancing Dream
Oil, 16" x 20"

My Dancing Dream

What is a prophecy
but what we ourselves call into being? The child

       watches the playful dancers
       flowing swirling shape shifters

wondering what life holds. Will the world
be the nurturing place

       she hears about in fairy tales
       grass bending in the breeze

sails shaking to the song of sea?
spider's silken whisper from the web?

       Or will the green below vanish
       in fire, downpour and pollution
       an ashen mist on the sea's face
       the sky veering ominous grey?

Daydreamers

Two enigmatic women
their Botticelli beauty

looms undeniable.
Like the butterfly

they long to glide away
their earth in tatters.

Floating between blood
and a wrathful world naked

the woman on the left more skeptical
than the calmer other woman

they grieve the loss of the linden tree
and celebrate the creeping in the dust.

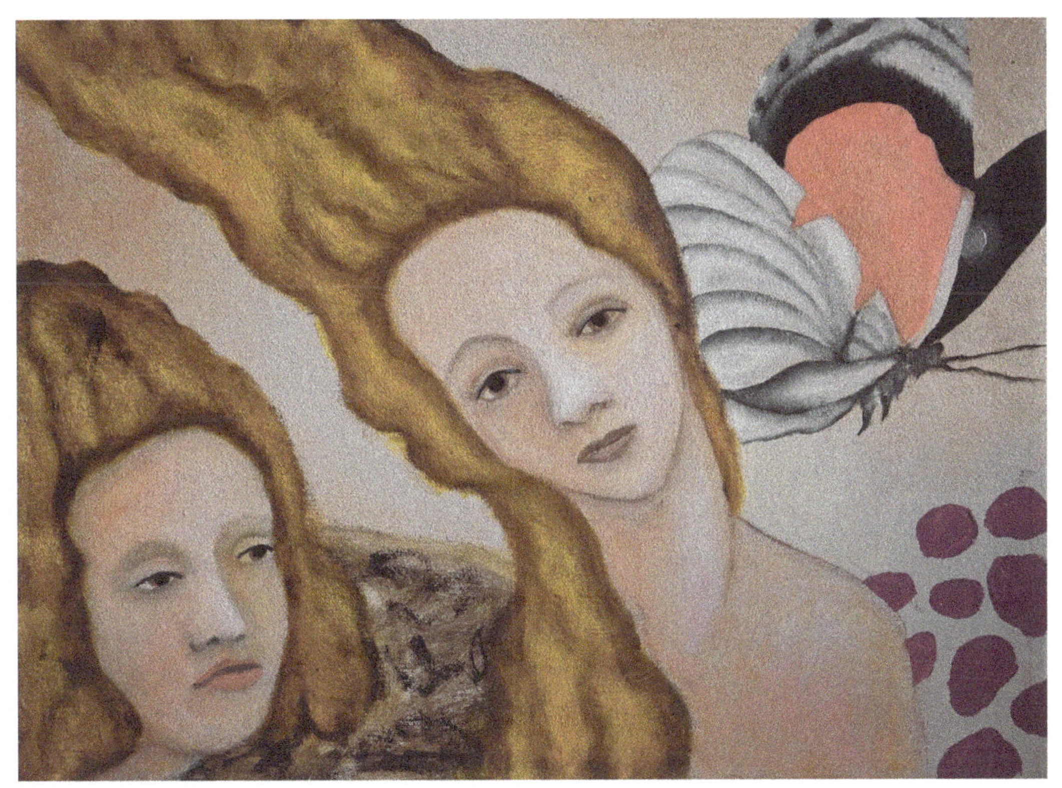

Daydreamers

Oil, 16" x 20"

Dreaming Venice

to fathom the terrain
of what is happening behind the mask
the darker questions
of the charade

we set out to explore it
the mystery behind the white curtain
the unwritten story
of the woman imagining herself
hair dripping
into the water city

together we board the gondola
and navigate the shifting paths
through the canals of Venice
we go

because what we know keeps changing
because what we refuse defines us
because obsessions in the dark of night
have unforeseen consequences

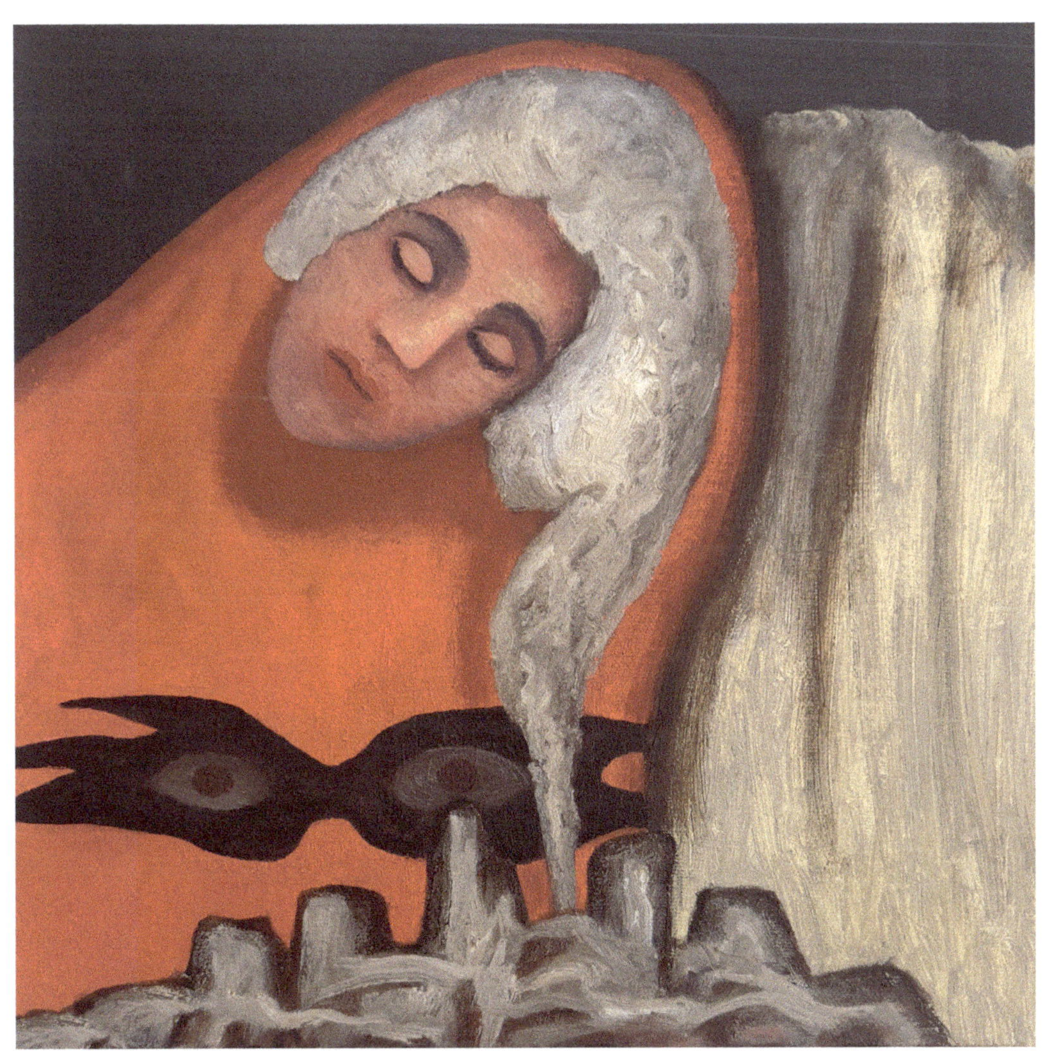

Dreaming Venice

Oil, 12" x 12"

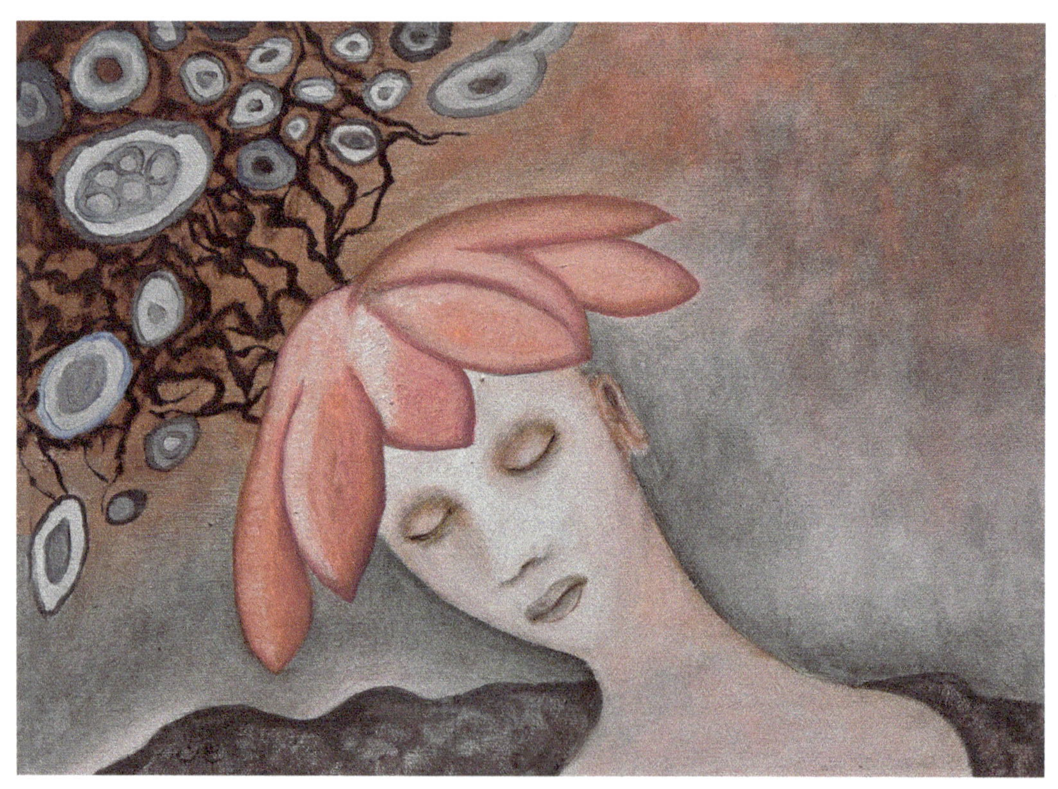

Lotus Dreamer

Oil, 12" x 16"

Lotus Dreamer

There is not one universe of the dream
only the specifics
like a crushed-winged bird trying to fly.

The lotus flower blossoms and drops a seed
by the rising of the sun. It closes at nightfall.

Buddha's plant survived the Ice Age
safe in its orbit atmosphere, rebirthing
each day in strength and purity.

>She imagines an instinctive planet
>a green, budding world.   Lodged
>in muddy waters, grey rain abounding.

>She awakens
>moving to well-lit wisdom
>the hesitant delicacy of the whole.

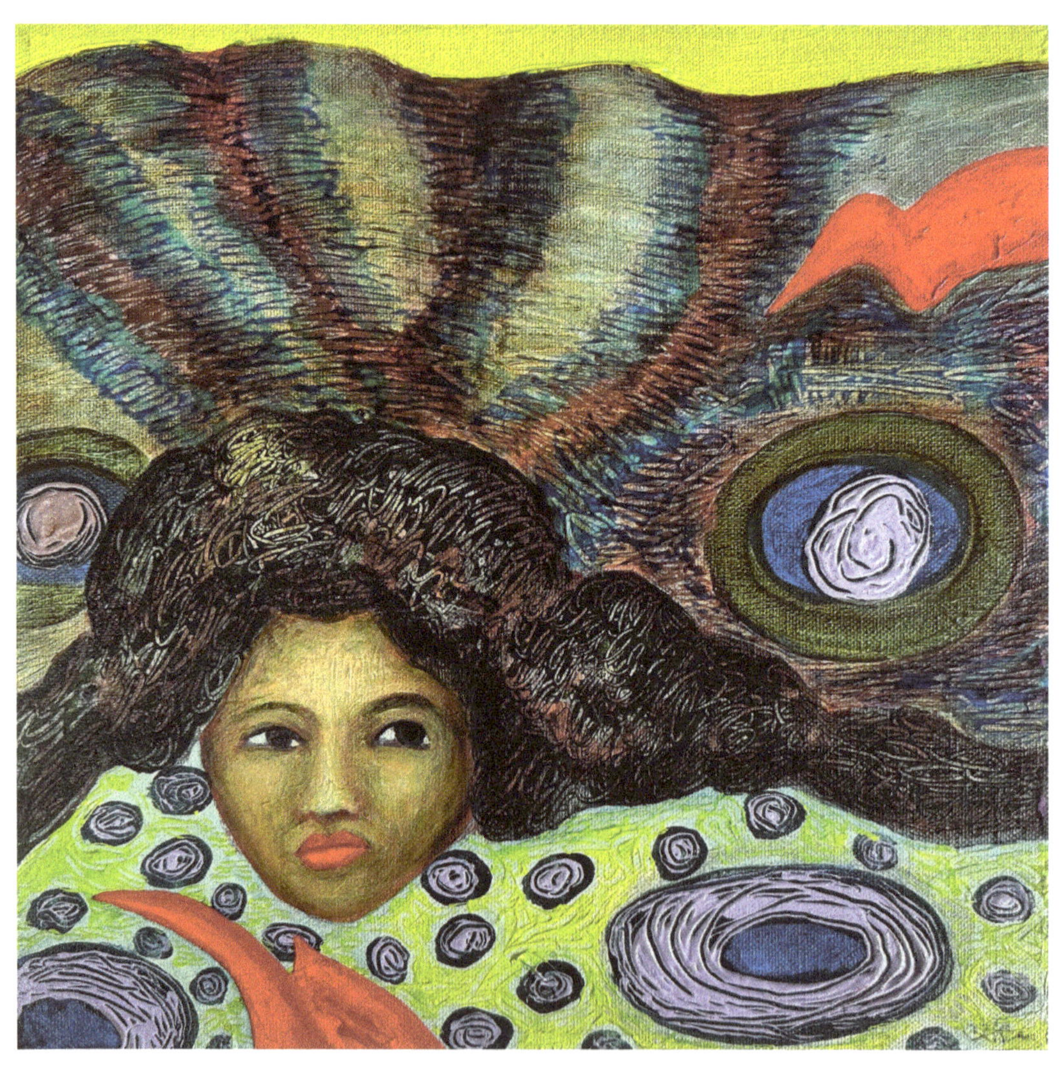

Guardian of Dreams
Oil, 12" x 12"

Guardian of Dreams

the guardian has no power
alert to our wistful whispers
her black lingering hair scatters
through landmarks that form our present

hopeless the beauty of the rare
the guardian has no power
below a multicolor sky
without sound, dialect, or light

drifting rocks fly with no purpose
she floats through the indigo night
the guardian has no power
greenery left to red flashes

seedling of desires she holds me
cradle and boneyard grow dour
the wish has long been forsaken
the guardian has no power

Deer Guardian

Your head and voice detach.
Antlers float in a red cloud
above the oozing earth.

What has happened to the deer?
Shrubs push up through tortured soil.

Rocks agitate to interlink with land.
Ferns perch on fluent, fluid blood.

Mountains parch with inflamed light.
Sky ages indifferent to the smoke
of previous landscapes.

The ancient pair below
watch their cosmos unravel.
How can they reconnect
the human, the more than human, and the earth?

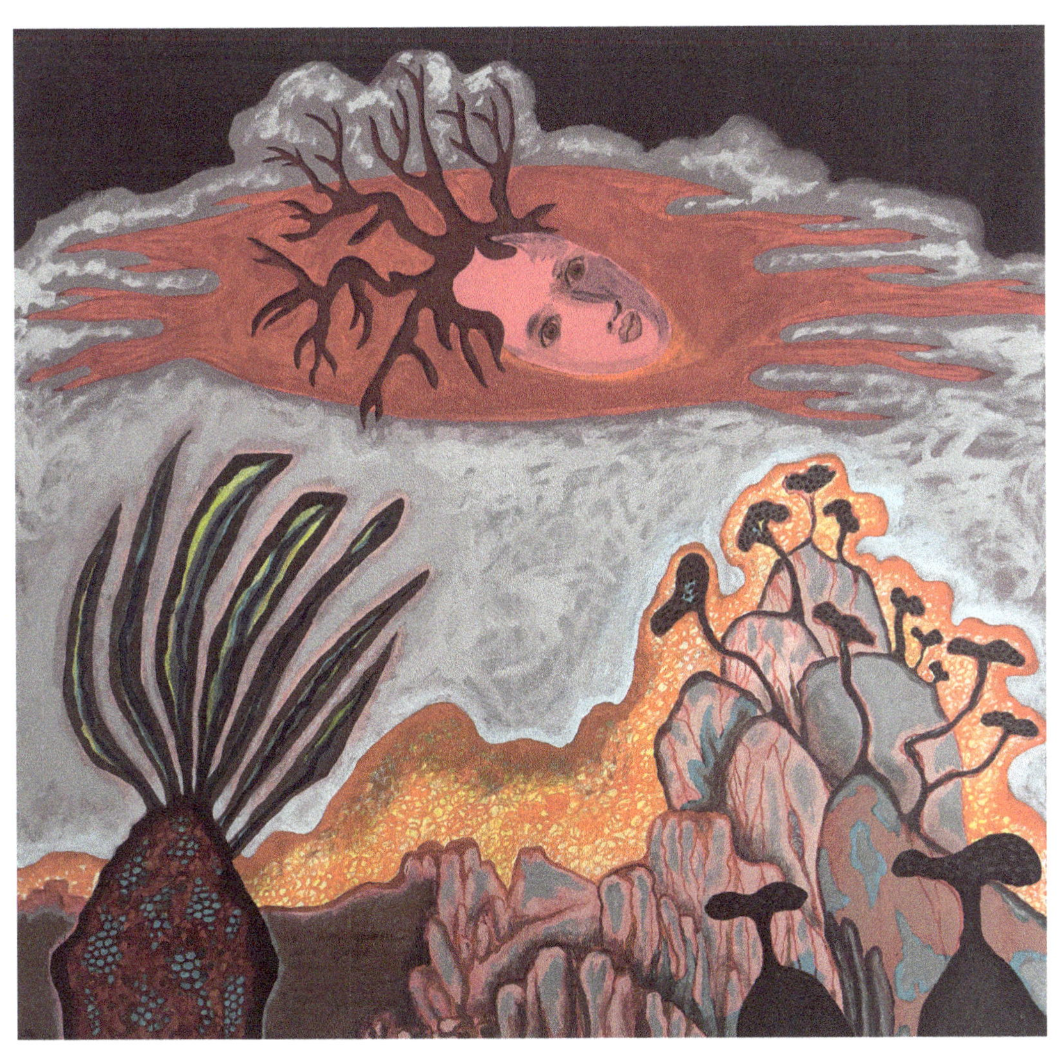

Deer Guardian
Acrylic, 36" x 36"

Mindscape of the Night

The demon battles the terrain
dueling a roulette wheel
gambling the world's extinction.
Death's distillation
scavenges shadowy shapes
lifeless branches of cypress.

Over each other
some attempt to escape.
They fall unable to keep up.
Purple air above.
Green growing verdure below
while the devil's fire creeps.

Suspended on the slopes
fluttering crown flashes.
The artist sees
the nightmare of the poisoned earth
leaving her breathless, frightened.
Can she defend herself?
Can she endure?
Can anything survive?

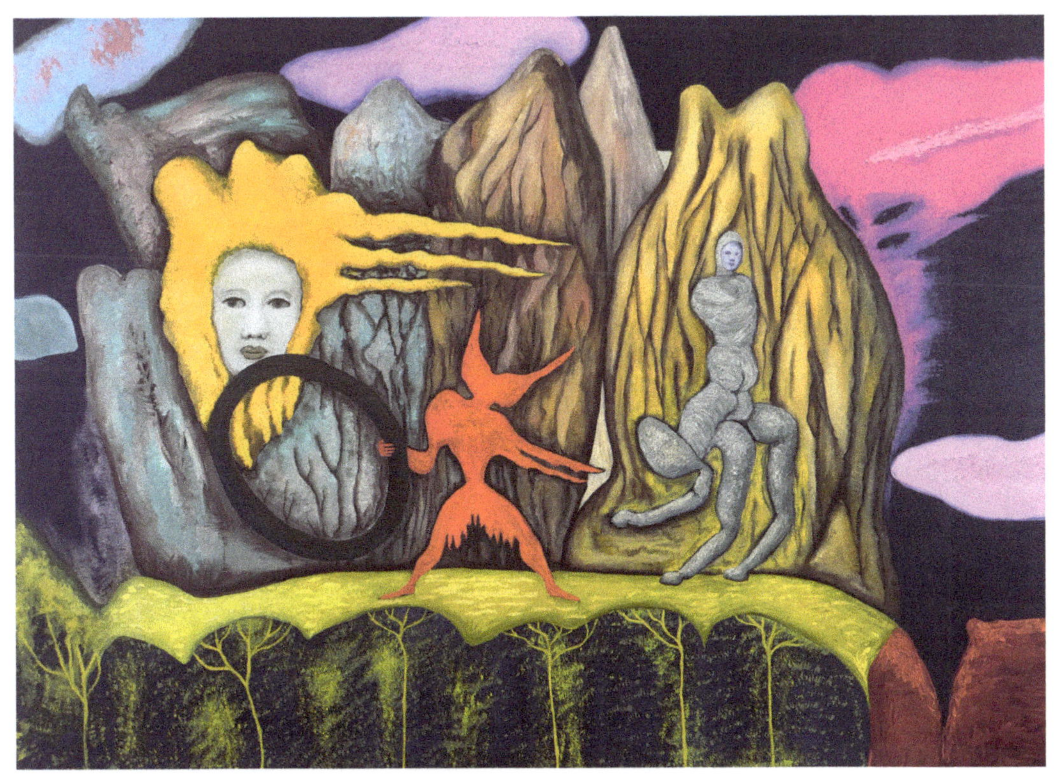

Mindscape of the Night

Oil, 36" x 48"

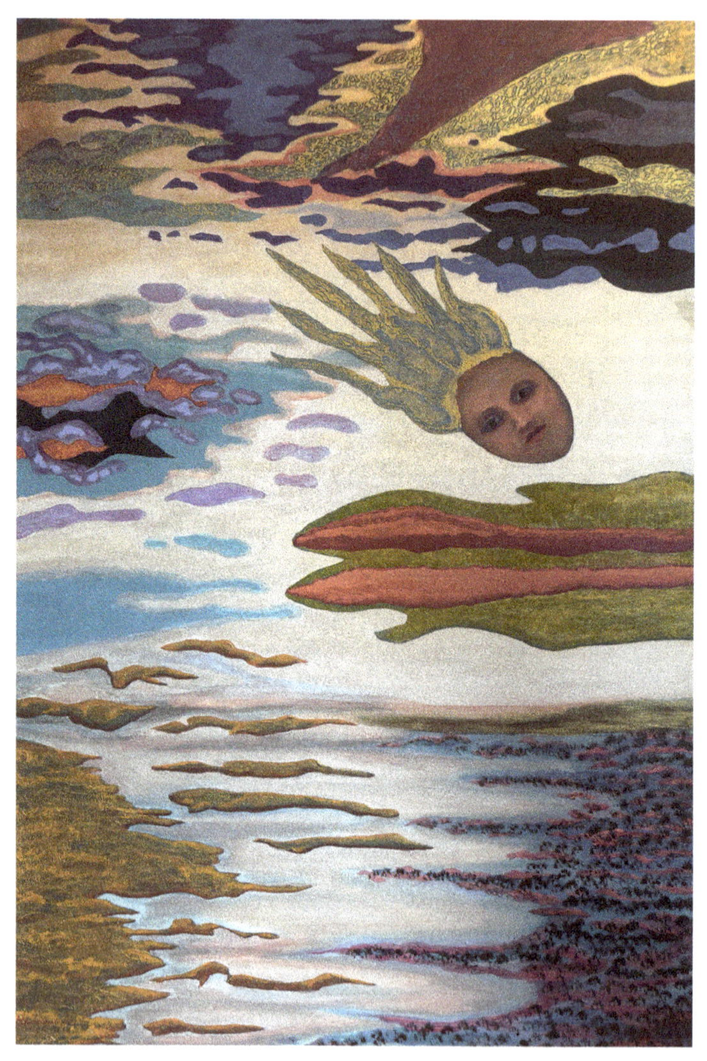

The Day Wavers between Going and Staying

Oil, 36" x 24"

The Day Wavers between Going and Staying

the day does not know where to go
pollution raids transient clouds
head hovers without permanence
water pushes into dense land

sunset skirmishes with color
the day does not know where to go
sky exudes purple red warning
wind surprises the woman's hair

country vanishes under sea
cloud beasts survey for asylum
the day does not know where to go
birds fly seeking to get away

earth cries to the heavens for help
fowls look for a place to put down
water courses flooding the land
the day does not know where to go

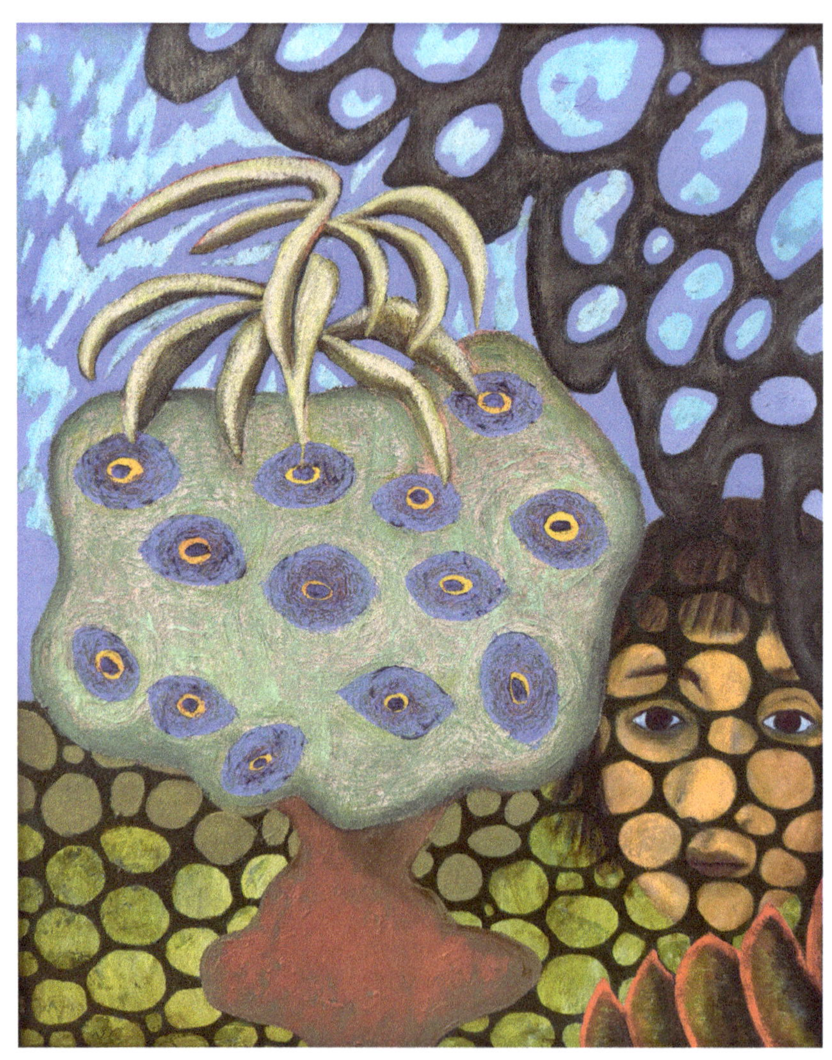

Young Woman

Oil, 20" x 16"

To Be That Young

The last of the water creatures
dances on the eyes
as the young woman sinks below.

      She ponders the why of everything
      on her five-fingered hand
      compressed in blood.

Six-pack rings
cut sharp into her face
dragging her down to the ocean floor.

      Rocks and dying coral
      hold her still
      plasma supports condemning eyes
      that wound her psyche
      and tangle her mind.

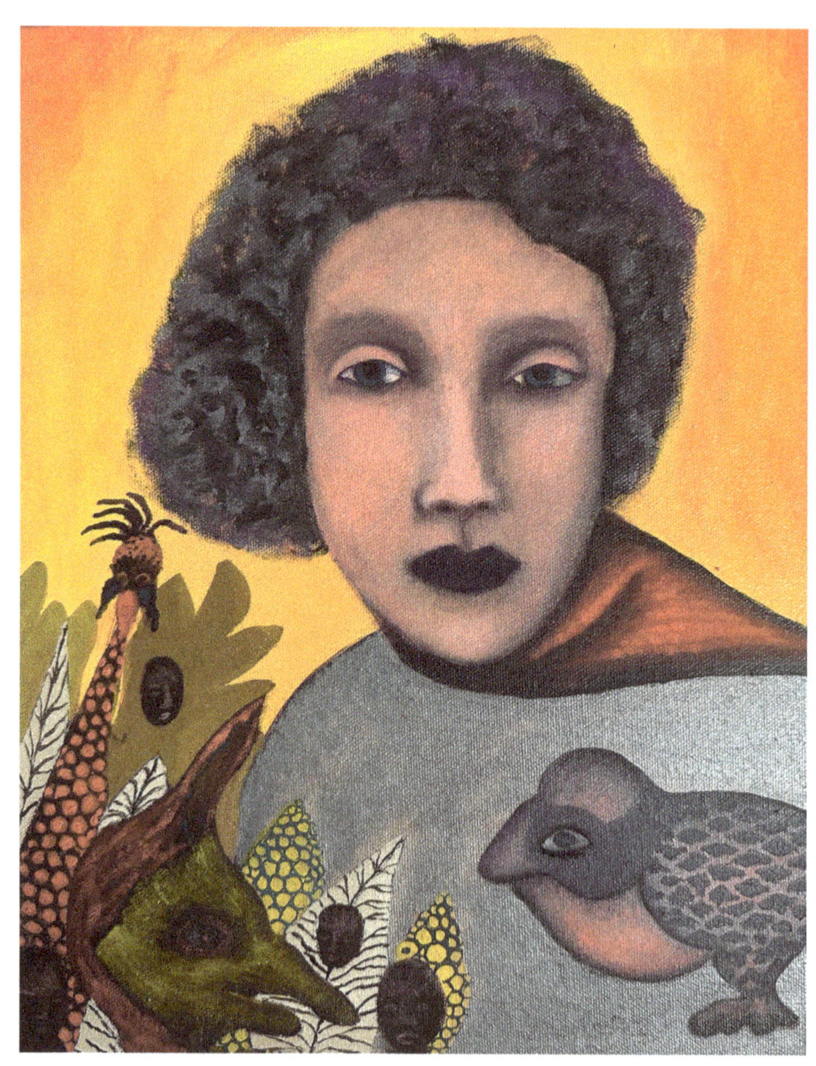

Yesterday

Oil, 16" x 12"

She Occupies Time

no quiet merging with the azure
but an orange sky earth
bizarre with diasporic life
bugs consume blossoms

still leaves fly forgetting giddy dance
before they reach the ground

fowl strange in beak and being
stand silent of chirps
malformed heads waiting
sporting jagged mandibles

at attention emaciated birds
abandon their flapping flight

waiting with heart spinning
she drifts above the world

where birds can't fly
where sleep stares
where hope conceals despair
under blue canvas

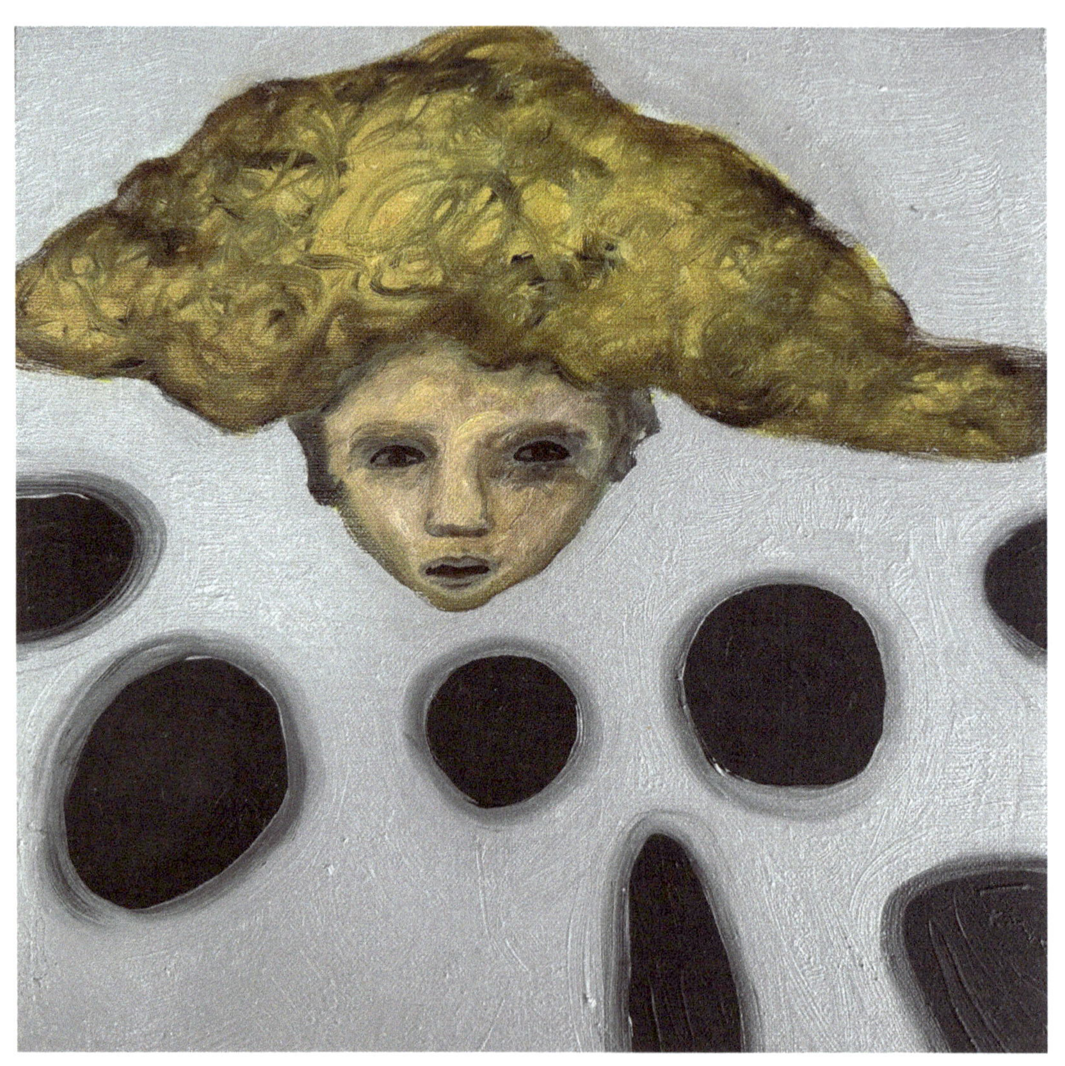

Child of 1000 Years

Oil, 12" x 12"

What World Will We Leave Her?

The child of 1000 years glides
disembodied her hair flowing
over a black earth.
What world will we leave her?

Draw a little closer.
Touch her cheek,
and you will see a sweet child,
no different than you or yours.

But the child of 1000 years knows the earth is dying.

Have we forsaken beauty
forfeited her birthright
forgotten the look of dry land
of light without merciless heat
flying sea fires in her sight
a million broken shards of mourn?

Will the frost, fog, dust disturb her air?
Will she feel a grass carpet beneath her bare feet?
Will the spring peepers sing her to sleep?
Will the lavender lilacs smell of home?
Will she taste the bananas split from the frond?
Will the fish fly above her bow?
Will she nurture children to carry on the world we leave her?

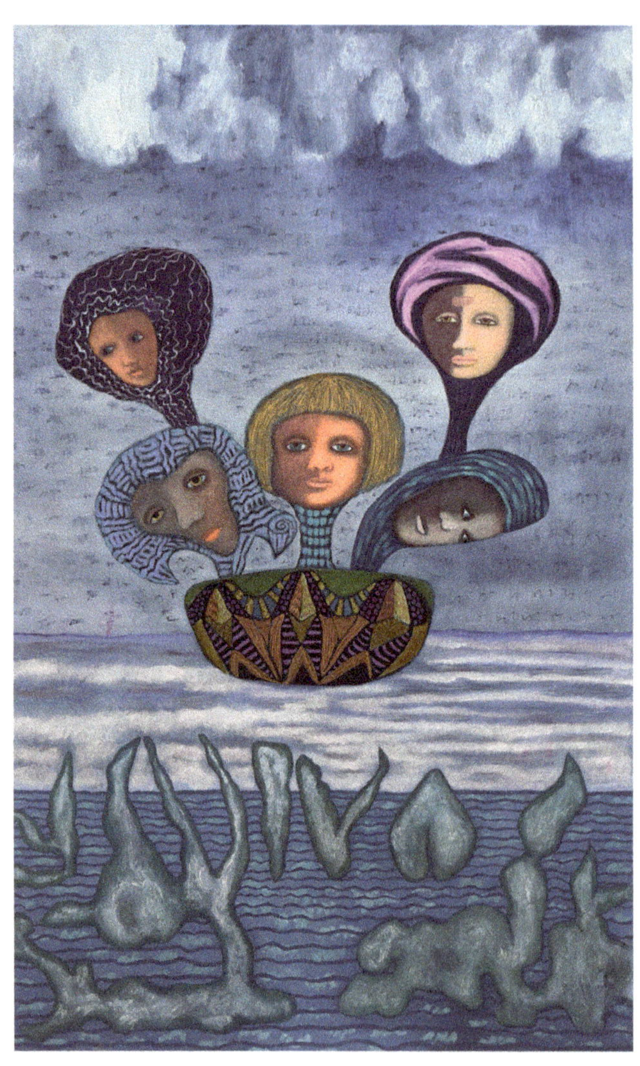

Perilous Journey

Oil, 60" x 36"

Perilous Journey

two things at once: the heads of five women and ocean

ocean unabetted by moonlight caresses
ocean that defeats the land
ocean that erodes rocks

floods destroy their homes and food
sea menace reaches up to block their passing clouds
a miserable grey, waiting to pounce their flight

        steadfast refugees, different colors, yet the same
        precariously perched
        navigating from danger to a new home

I want to write this poem so it swallows the excess water of the world
I want to write this poem so the colors embrace the words
I want to write this poem so all people land a place on this earth
I want to write this so the women journey to safety and I disappear into this poem

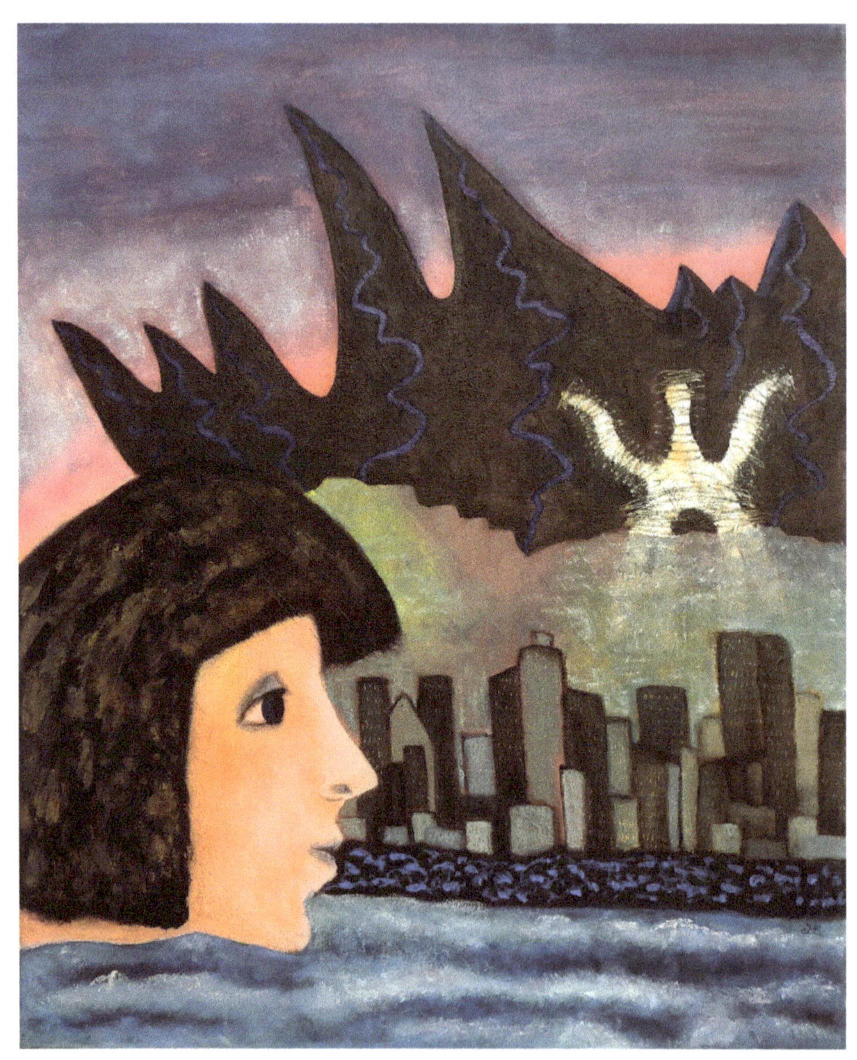

The Blue Line
Oil, 20" x 16"

Blue Line

Does she think the city will survive
the rising water
filling the offices,
subways, sewers, streets?

Does she still run in Central Park?
Go to lunch at the Grand Hyatt?
Have a drink in Bryant Park?
Watch standup at the Gotham Club?

The Big Apple's core emerges
floating above New York City,
a thwarted alien, a severed body
above 250 million tons of concrete.

Alarming sky the color of petrified plums
against a tired wall
cassocked in future blood
drapes a swineherd pink that once blended with pure air.

Spiked mountain's wastewater confounds
the steel buildings' structure.
Putrid smog silences
the aviary choruses.

Does she think she can cross the blue line
despite the heat, stench, flood,
hitting her stride in time to escape
on wings of desire?

Red Wall

Red blood, boundaries, lips. The wall
blocks the woman.

Windows offer the possibility of escape,
six curtainless stained glass pieces

Tree between the woman and the wall,
blocks the windows. Snow keeps land
lifeless. Winter plants gather at the
woman's throat, waiting to come back,
floating, perhaps dead.

Head in the forefront,
other body parts in peril.

Hair forms a helmet.
How many obstacles does the woman face?

Wall, winter, lifeless shrubs.
She transforms her emotional life
to the landscape without smile.
She battles for the possibility of spring,
kinship of family, children, other women.
Alone and strong, she longs for roses and redemption.

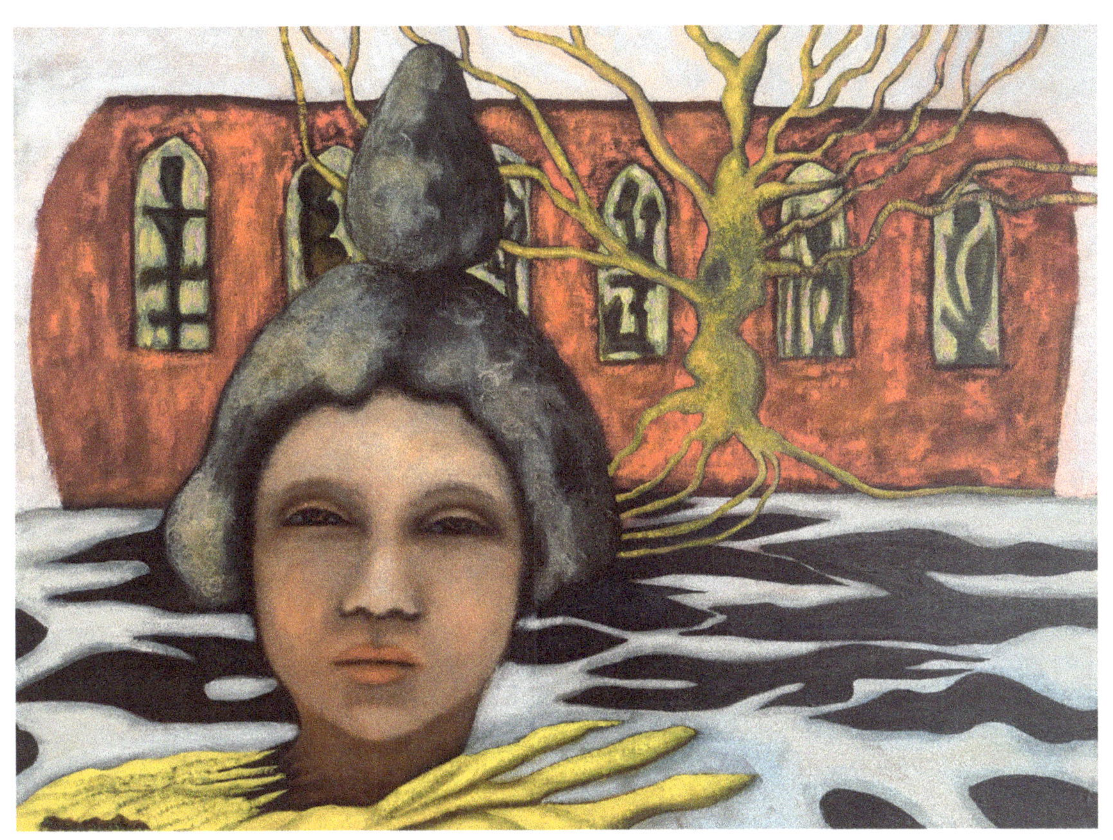

The Red Wall

Oil, 18" x 24"

Nature Remains Our Home

Dear Floating Woman:

You grow green plants with red light.
Hovering at the center, you become Mother Earth.

Plants emanate from your head.
Seeds plentify and propagate.
Vines multiply in the air.

Nature remains our home.
We must feel the coolness of the water.
We must hear the quiet of the wood.

I want to be there with you.
I want to grow seeds and fruit.
I want to be an oak planted in the dirt.

Sincerely,
The Poet

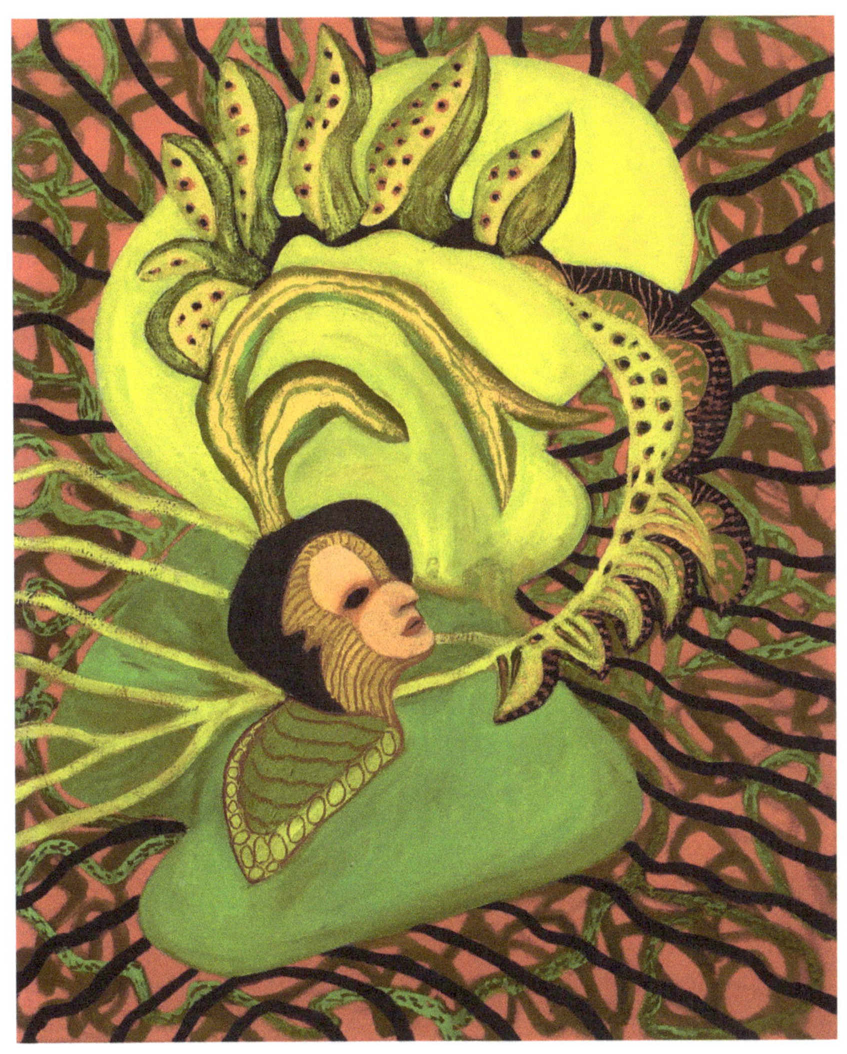

Nature Is Our Home

Oil, 20" x 16"

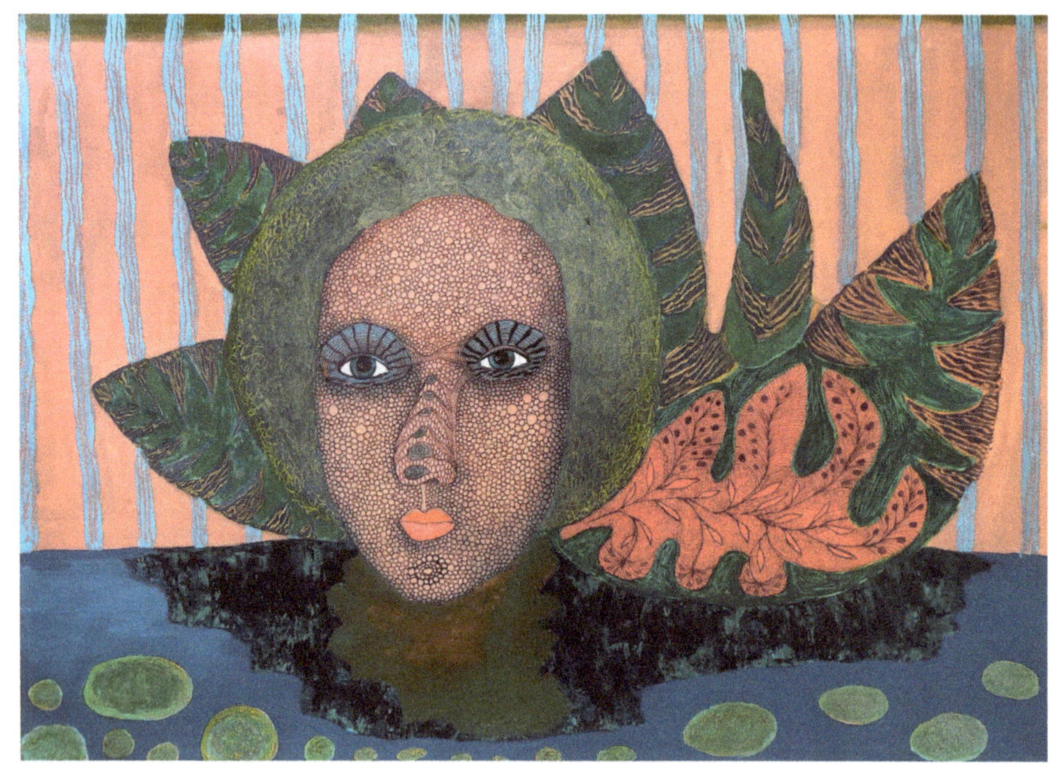

I Feel Close to Nature Too
Acrylic, 22" x 30"

The Closeness of Nature

I want to be close to nature
earth travels in the torrid sky
green foliage expands my hair
mountains burst forth my surface skin

when you trample on me I yell
I want to be close to nature
my eyes cultivate blue seashells
my face erodes sand from the shore

polluted ground battles
smoke and oil choking in a candy corn sky
I want to be close to nature
fighting the smog and toxic waste

a firedrake dragon swallows the shrubs
alive in the forest
charging planet beast must persevere
I want to be close to nature

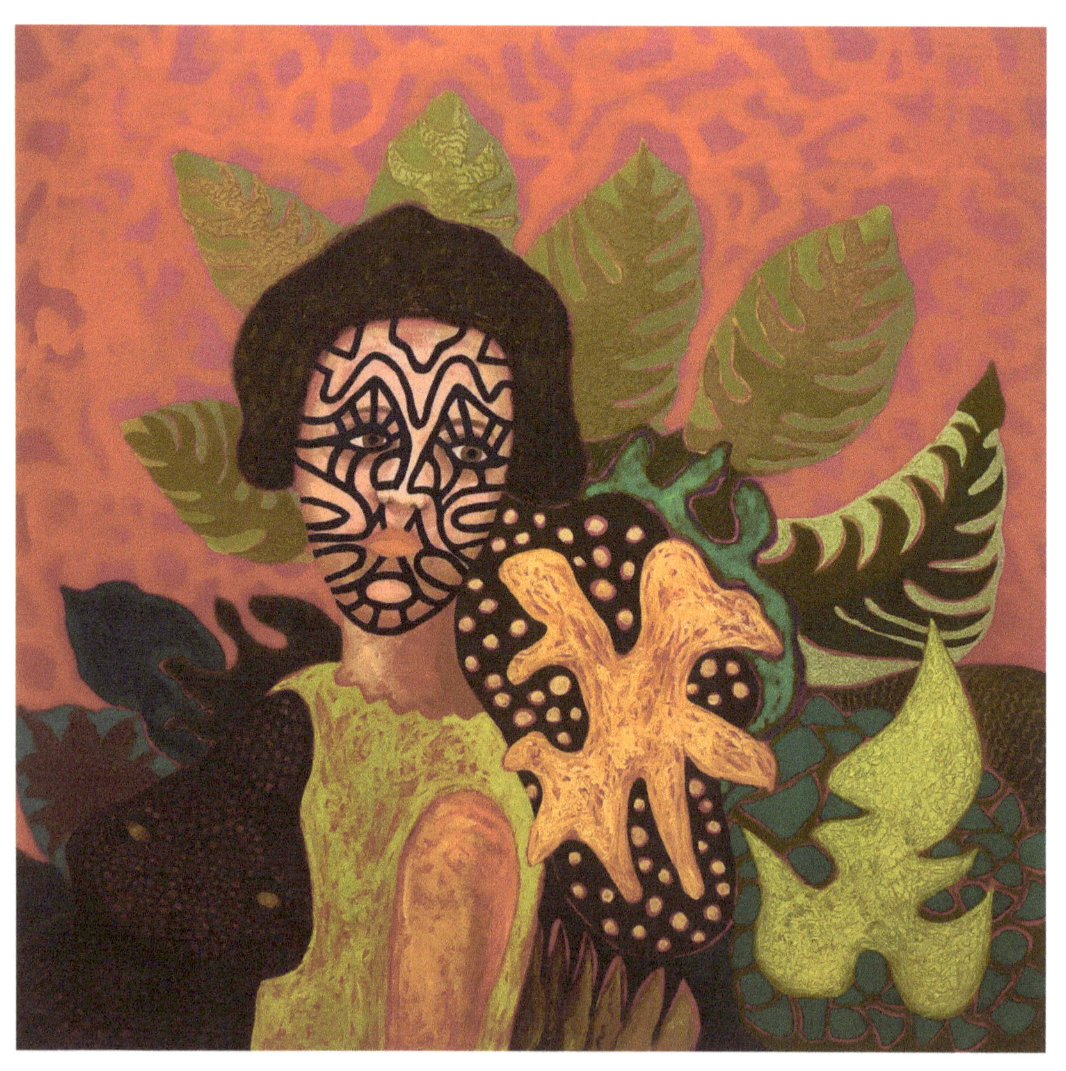

Māori Woman

Oil, 40" x 40"

Māori

Mystical memory grows
the moko from her heart
as it appears on her face.
This ancient art form
chisels into her skin,
smudges carved lines,
and enhances her knowledge.
She weaves her fate carefully.
Bone and music
guide her face marks
to solemnize her passage.

In the spiritual realm,
her ancestors know her symbols
and heal them with kōpi tree balm.

She moves forward with tomorrow
to save the kauri tree broadleaf
and the tuakara lizard
to do what she can
to save the ailing earth.

Queen of the Woods

Your presence majestic
stepchild of an embattled earth.
Sylvan spirit
clothed with plants crowned
with a mosaic halo. Woodland deity

with fiery-treed antennas
your leaf-bordered tale more picturesque
than my words. Your desolate

estate, down-trodden forest, bleak skies
anticipate your sadness. To what
mountain altar do you come? What planet
palace awaits you in these hills?

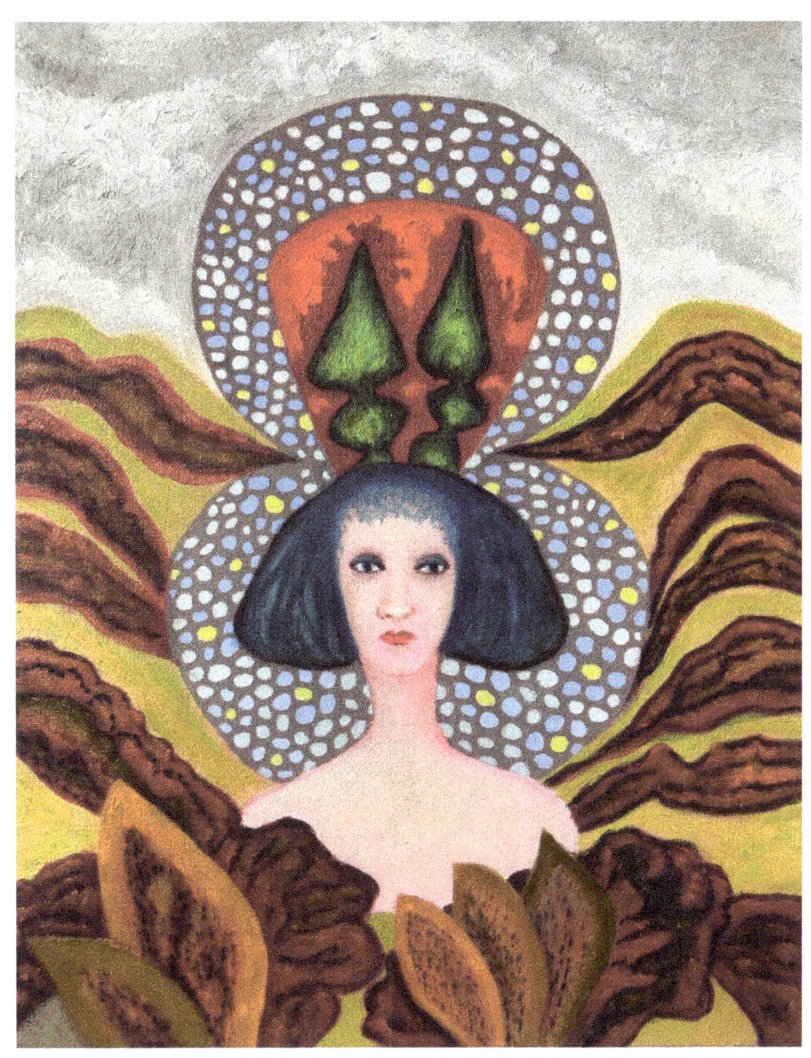

Queen of the Woods

Oil, 20" x 16"

Wandering Queen

The queen's head floats high and sees all
with her many eyes. Her crown
a lingering cloud. Her sons and daughters
wait. She wants to protect her children
from earth's destruction.

The troll has taken
all the trees from the mountains
and leaves only the blood-stained plants.
Shrubs struggle to grow
at the edge of the mountains.

The lady guards the hills from further damage.
She protects the fjords, the gateway
to the fabled world.
Northern lights loom ominously
through the fire in the sky.

What happens to the nomadic royal?
Will she save her family?
Will she have another
born between her legs
in the new world,
the mythical planet?

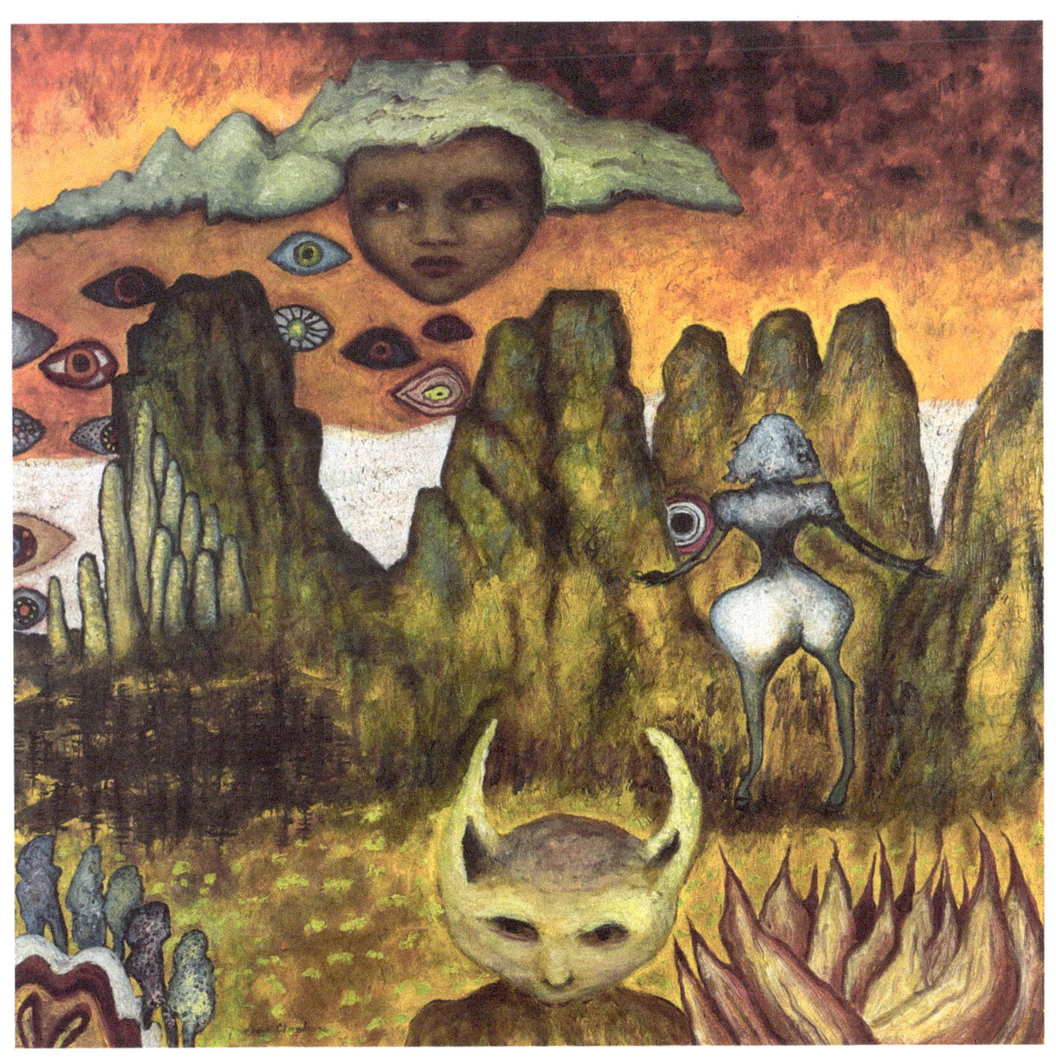

Wandering Queen

Oil, 24" x 24"

Artemis

I am the goddess of wild animals
by red or orange light

crocodiles lie in the mud hiding
from skulls waiting for them to die.

Wilderness ignites in fires
that burn all day destroying

my cypress trees as the blue sky
fights to shine through.

I am a warrior with philosophy and poetry
words are my weapon
they kill climate injustice
my quill wings swiftly soar
and make me fearless.

I am a silver dreamer
talisman believer
tablet carrier
passion breather. I float
above and below.

You may not see me
but listen
and you will hear
my voices rise.

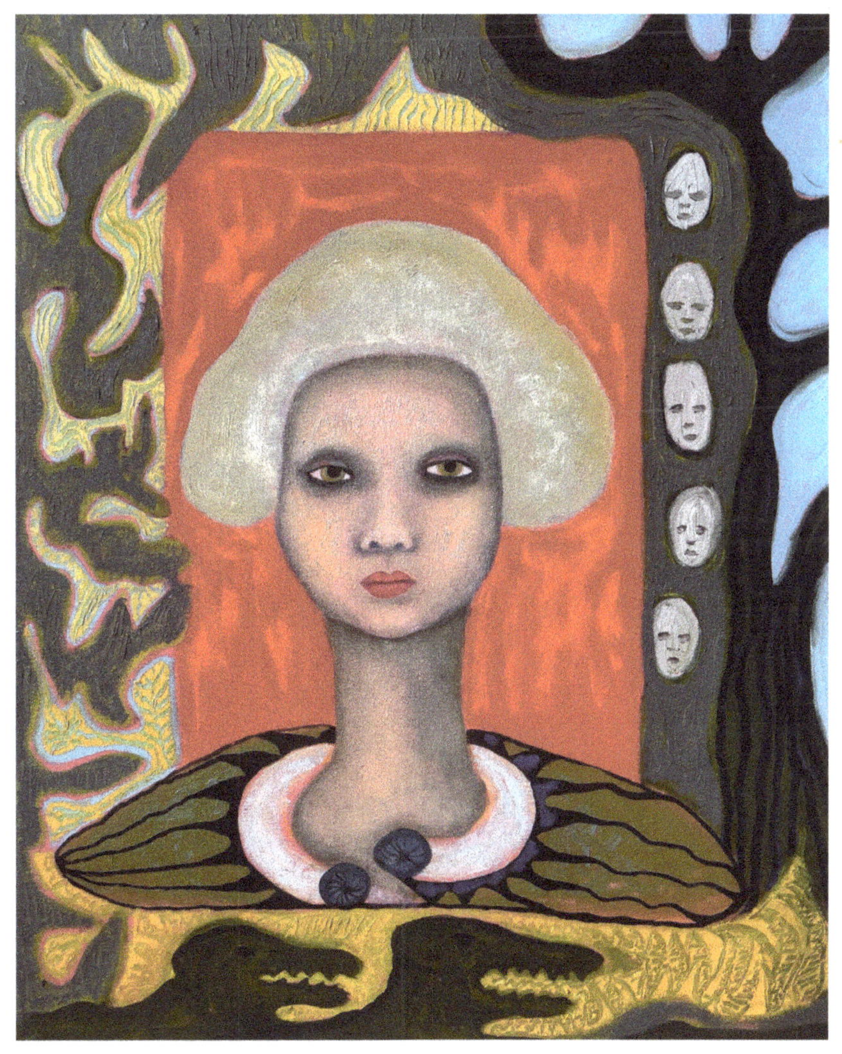

Artemis

Oil, 20" x 16"

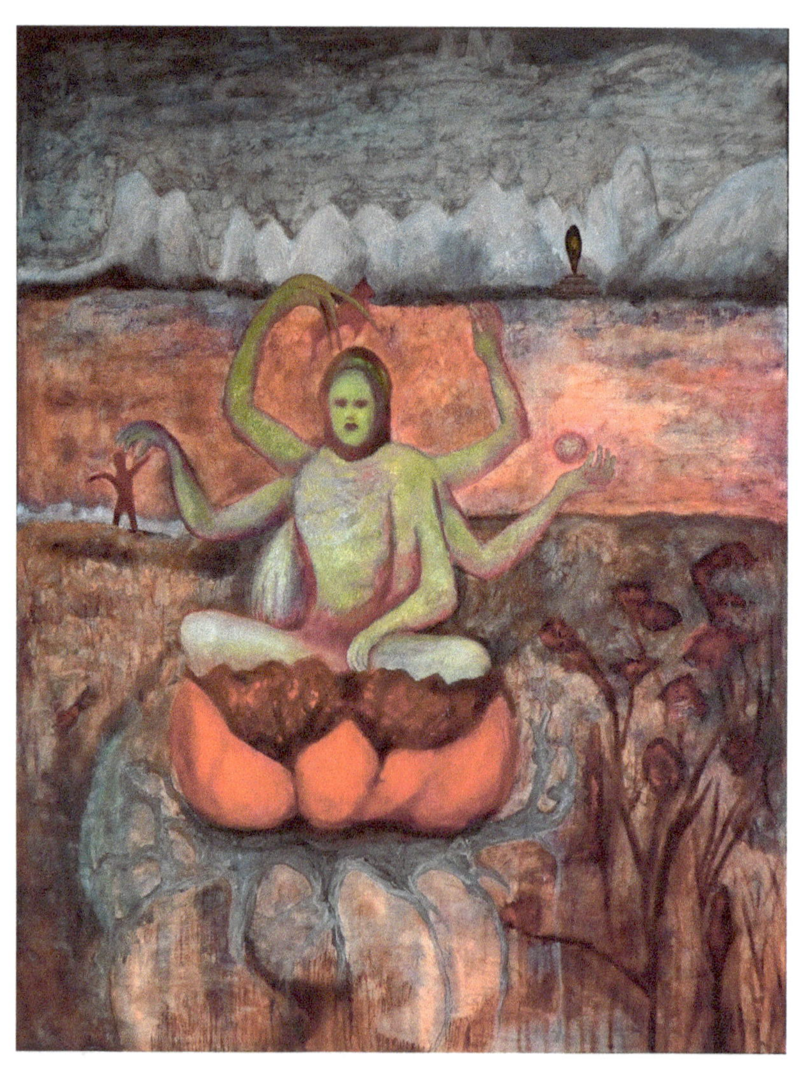

Lotus Goddess

Oil, 48" x 36"

Lotus Goddess

The green ochre of your face
against the pomegranate earth
makes you part of the whole.

This head covering highlights
the pain of your eyes. In your many arms
you hold a horse,
a ball, a human.
Another arm lost over
to peregrine falcon claws,
the tendrils of octopus lost
in the gems of the sea.

The icebergs melt behind you
revealing barren land.
Your scarlet lap sits
on a berry-vine lotus.

You are two goddesses twirling to balance:
The mother of truth growing the morning calm
and the dancer who crushes all things.
You hold the future in your many hands.

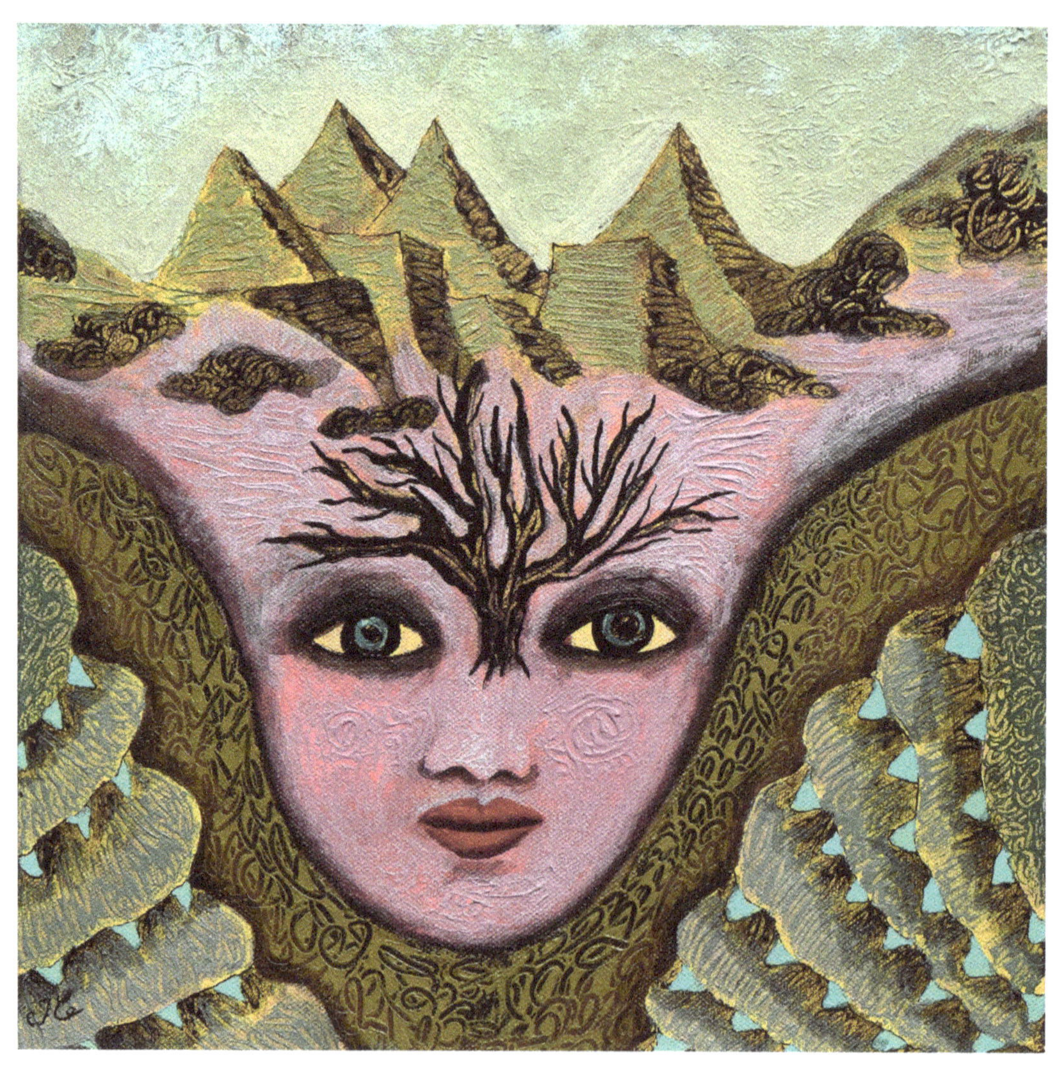

The Goddess Speaks

Oil, 12" x 12"

The Goddess Speaks

The goddess lives
inside these mountains. You continue
to climb to the top
looking up seeing
nothing but mottled heavens. Into the hole

you plunge but there lies
no single collective mind.
The goddess questions you
about losing the azure of her sky. She sees

the bareness of her trees
almighty guardians ones
that used to give shade to swallows
and creatures of the woods.

Her thoughts spread threads
on wheel-centered spokes.

What if the birches don't blossom,
shaking out their brown-leaved hearts?
What if the thrushes are banished from song,
voices split from their throats?

Give my trees the grant of green again, she cries,
let the birds sing toward heaven.

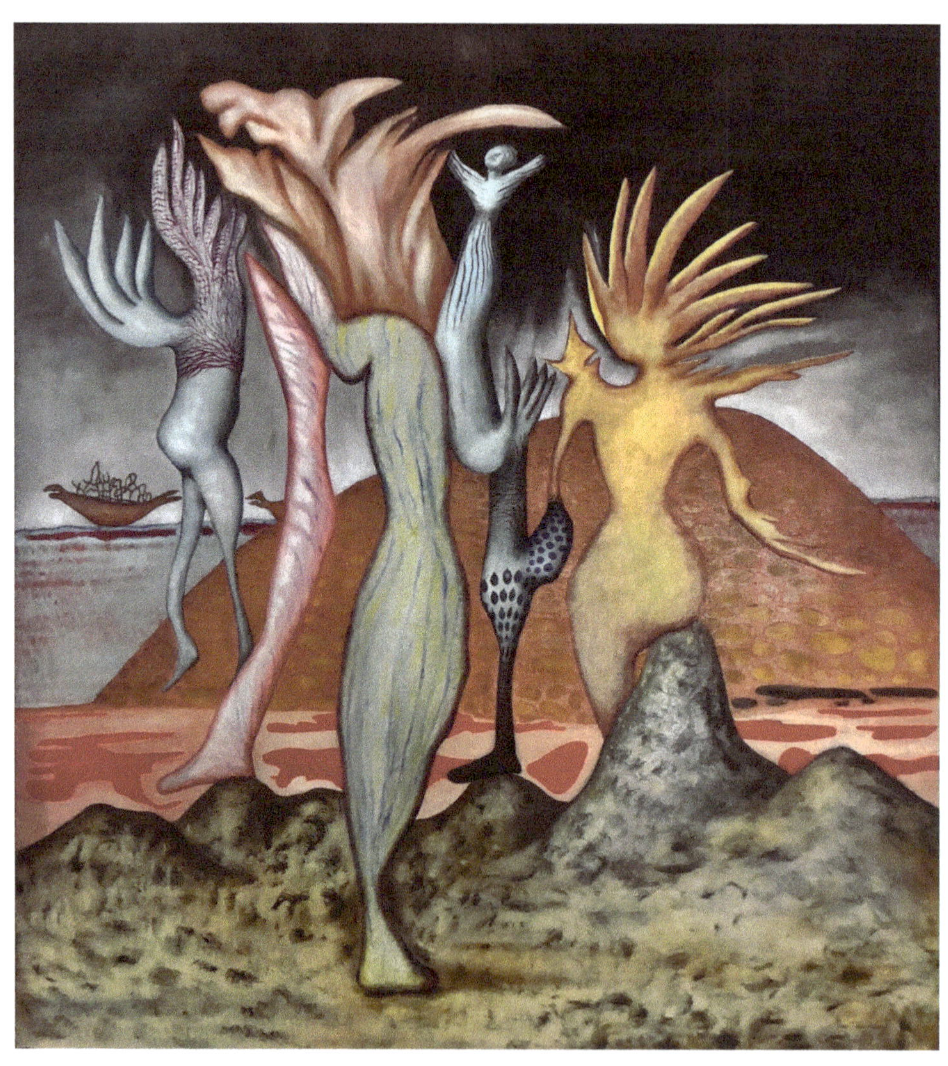

Ino

Oil, 54" x 48"

Ino and the Goddesses

The golden goddess sits
on a rock watching. The flying deity
stands in praise, blood covering one wing. Ino
raises her hands in supplication
to the ancient ones
for her water kingdom.

She prays
for the aquatic animals to heal
the fish to flow
the waters to purify.

Blood runs on the ground from the mountain. A boat
filled with people flees the polluted water. The goddesses
remain grounded in their hope knowing
that their wishes may come
that the seas see everything
that nothing will come to pass
without the blessing of the ancestors
without a vision of a better future.

Between Shell and Troll

Artist's divination:
she visions the earth's end.
Heaven-wheel keeps turning
through all the constellations.

High-spire shell. The illustrator
of the new world passes
through an open-ended canal
to the fjord the monster guards.

The painter
predicts the demise
of the forest. Fires will
destroy tree garlands.

Through the conch hunt
resonating vision echoes through hulks.
She clears troll and grey sky
and comes out whole on the other side.

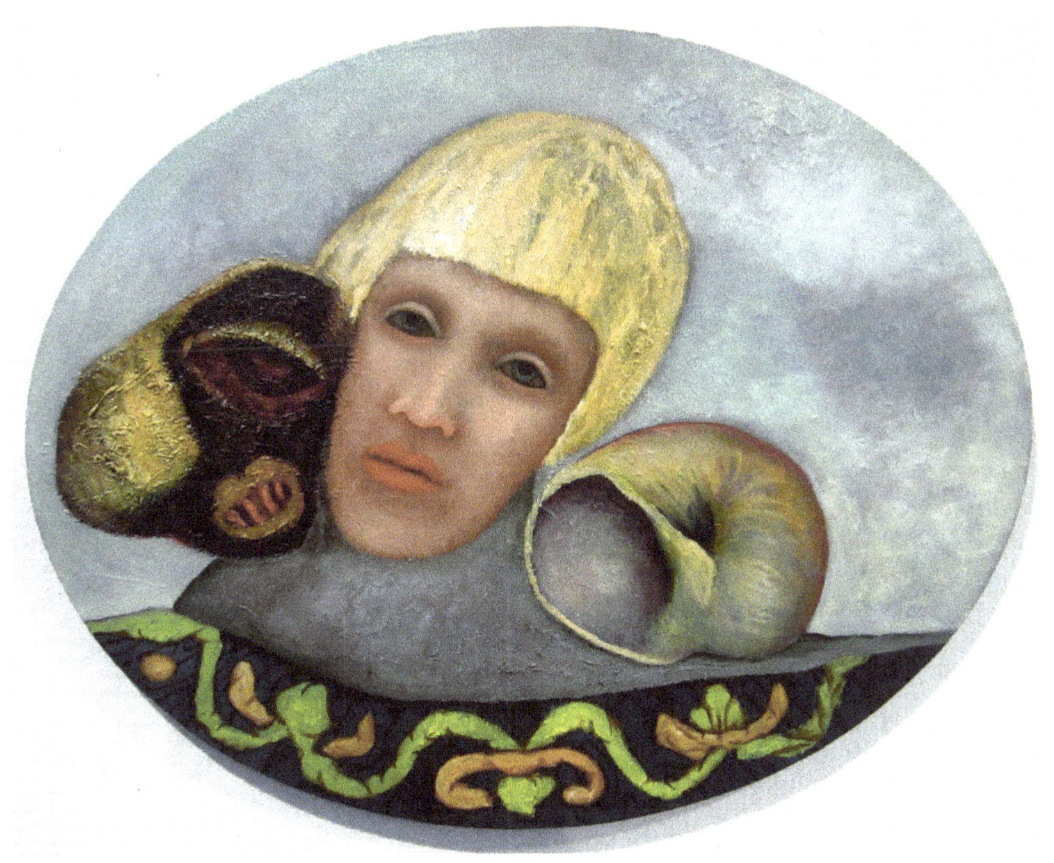

Between Shell and Troll
Oil, 16" x 20" (oval)

Looking to the Future

Here stands the Green Goddess of Nature,
looking at a crystal ball with crimson tears.
Bear remembers sunshine's fresh face.
Cat carries the remains of a mummified sphinx.

Here stands the Green Goddess of Nature.
Glaciers dissolve into rocks.
Mountains host dead branches. In memory
trees float high above.

Here stands the Green Goddess of Nature.
Mourning dove perches behind the temple
waiting in fierce belief of scarlet faith
for a blooming eternity.

Here stands the Green Goddess of Nature,
banishing grey-skulled trolls
seeking warm caves in the woods
knowing the ancestors sleep within.

Egypt drowns in the Nile. Lotus heart
beats with the tides. Eyes copy
the curve of the waves. They hope for
a planet in harmony.

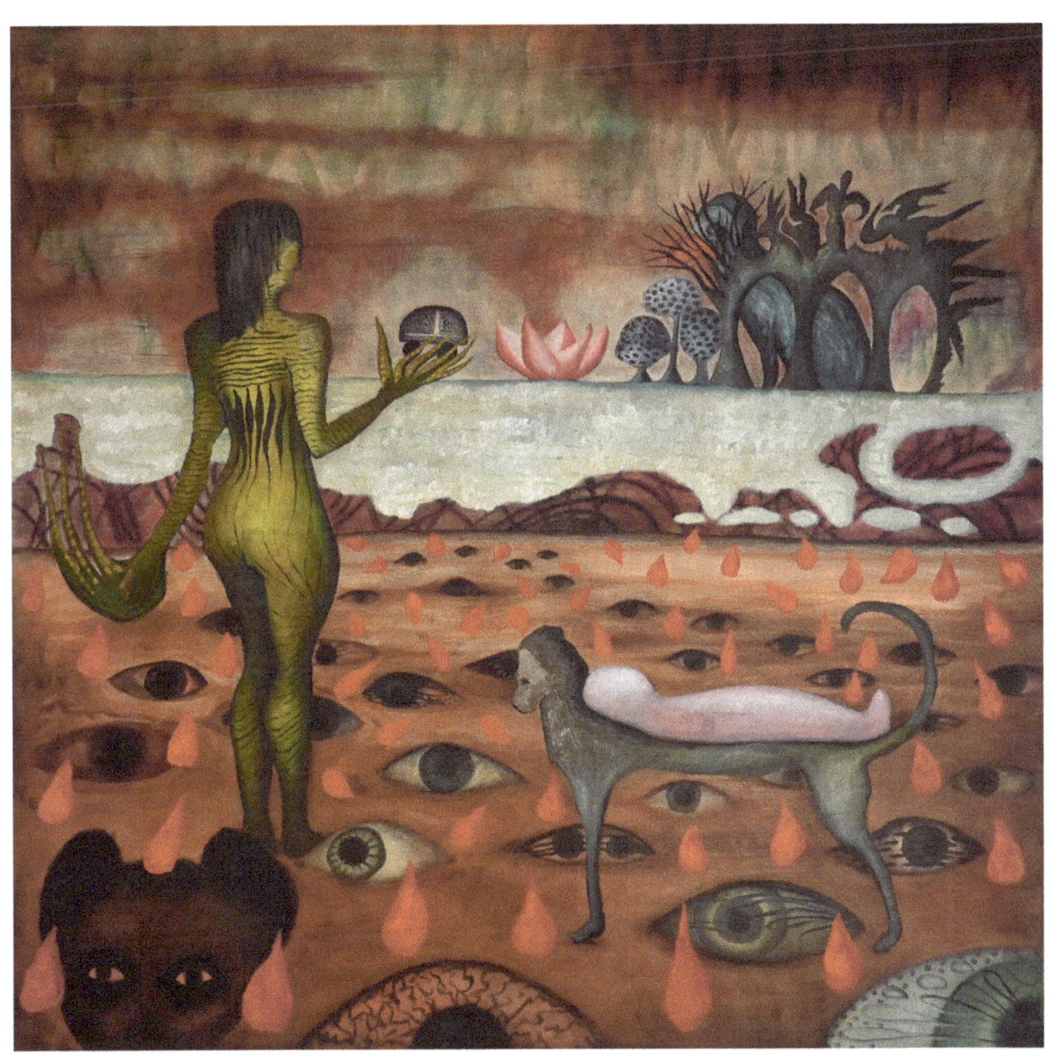

The Eyes Have It
Oil, 42" x 42"

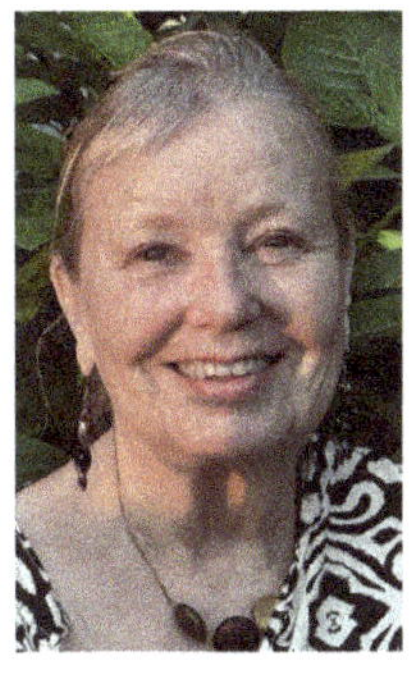

IRENE CHRISTENSEN divides her time between New York City and Oslo, Norway, producing her work in her studios. She has exhibited in Europe, Asia, South America, and the United States. Her art has been shown in museums, art centers, and galleries in the United States, Costa Rica, Norway, Germany, Belgium, Brazil, Israel, and Argentina. She showed an installation of nine accordion books at Palazzo Mora during the Venice Biennale. She has received many honorariums and awards in Europe and the United States and is represented in many museums and private collections. John Zeaman, art critic and writer, says, "Irene Christensen's art is about painting as a magical act."
• www.irenechristensen.art

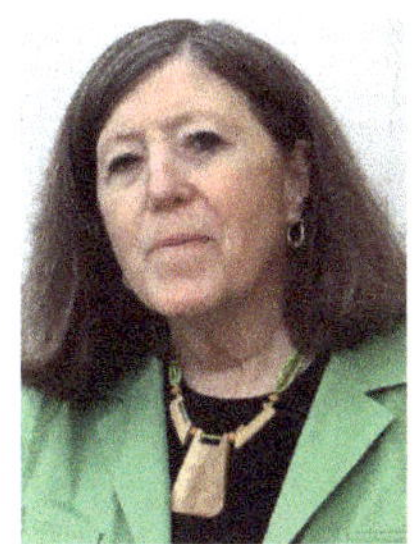

EILEEN P. KENNEDY is the author of two collections of poetry: *Banshees* (Flutter Press, 2015), which was nominated for a Pushcart Prize and won Second Prize in Poetry from the Wordwrite Book Awards; and *Touch My Head Softly* (Finishing Line Press, 2021), which Literary Titan has described as "emotionally-charged poetry that explores life with observant poems that will appeal to anyone who loves inspired poetry." It was a finalist for the International Book Awards in General Poetry. She taught writing and literature on the faculty of the City University of New York. She lives in Amherst, Massachusetts, with the ghost of Emily Dickinson.
• www.eileenpkennedy.com

Shanti Arts

Nature ▪ Art ▪ Spirit

Please visit us online
to browse our entire book catalog,
including poetry collections and fiction,
books on travel, nature, healing, art,
photography, and more.

Also take a look at our highly regarded art
and literary journal, *Still Point Arts Quarterly*,
which may be downloaded for free.

www.shantiarts.com